Derek Jarman

Edited by

John Hansard Gallery

Alexandra Symons Sutcliffe *1994*

Under a table a four-year-old watches the adult world from the knee down, shoed feet moving across the wooden floor of a cottage by the sea. It's a birthday party, but as the child thinks all parties are for birthdays it is possible that she's misunderstood the occasion. As the night continues the movement of the feet becomes more erratic, and from the child's perspective – framed by the edge of a tablecloth – the world of the grown-ups destabilizes. She retreats further into the privacy of her own world, the noise of drunk people comforting her as much as it inhibits. Then, unexpectedly the face of her mother appears, reaching out and hooking the child under her armpits, lifting her from under the dividing and protecting barrier between the adult and child worlds, her mother says, "Come and say hello to Derek."

The sight of the man enthroned in a chair, wrapped in a blanket, throws off the assumption that this is a birthday party, it is not possible that this man could get any older or was ever young. Without any understanding of the situation a flight response sets off inside her, she's scared by the man's out-of-timeliness. By early 1994 Derek was very ill, he was blind, and the crudeness of the AIDS drug-cocktails had ravaged him almost as much as the virus itself. Now it is unusual to see someone so papery and noduled, but in the early nineties the by-proxy pox was a common side effect of treatment of the illness and left prickly moonscapes on people's cheeks.

Held on the hip, the child clamps her chubby knees to her mother's side, pushing the socket of her eye into the firm point of a shoulder. Sucking strands of hair into her mouth, grinding it between milk teeth, drawing out the taste of conditioner and sea salt, willing her mother to stop walking towards the man on the chair. Psychic protestation unheeded, she says loudly: "No mummy, I don't want to, he looks like a thistle." Her fear is understood, both by her mother and by the man, there is safety and understanding in the adult world after all and she is let go to return under the table, or look for her father, or find something sweet to eat.

Derek died a matter of weeks after the party. He was buried at St Clement's Church in Old Romney, an eleventh-century parish with a pastel pink interior, painted so for a live-action Disney production in the early 1960s. His burial plot is just at the edge of the branch span of a Yew tree, which as of 1988 was certified as being 560 years old. The headstone of his grave, large and black, reads 'Derek Jarman', and nothing else. Around a third of the entries to the church's guest book state the visitor came to see Derek's grave.

He died in February and Keith planted snow drops around his grave. After they blossomed a representative from the council informed Keith that floral tributes outside of the plot were not permitted and they needed to be removed which, unhappily, they were. A short time later a large and indignant thistle grew out of the middle of the grave, prickly, phallic, and obstinate, but within the legal perimeters of the

Old Romney guidelines on the use of burial plots. Botanic divination or a poetic coincidence the – now adult – child at the party has felt assured by the arrival of the thistle, a sign that it is possible to be understood.

Tilda Swinton *Artists live in houses*

Artists live in houses and make work in them. They make work in other people's houses, too.

There are countless plaques on countless walls across the globe running to catch up with the trail of inspired moments down the ages: 'here he wrote such and such'; 'between the years blank and blank, she completed so and so'; 'he lived here'; 'she boarded here'; even 'for a week/a night they slept here'.

Artists also work on the bus. In trains. In cafes and on the sides of roads, under trees and canvas and bedclothes by torchlight.

Let's maybe conclude that art is generated everywhere: this idea flicks a beautiful switch, in my view. It de-exoticises and brings closer the idea of artists' work, rubs it into the landscape of regular – lived – human life. This is closer to an accurate picture, as I know it to be. Artists: writers, painters, sculptors, filmmakers, performers, musicians, philosophers – make work within our lived days and in between the doorways of a social mortal span...

It would be impossible to catch, therefore, like a butterfly in a net, every site of every artist's creative inspiration.

Let's just say, that might be The World Itself, after all.

I first saw Prospect Cottage the day that Derek did.

We had driven down to find a bluebell wood to shoot in: I had remembered a wide bluebell expanse in Kent from my schooldays there. We pottered down in my ramshackle little car and found the idyll now covered in concrete. A little disheartened, we headed for the coast, abandoning bluebells in search of fresh air.

Derek's father had recently died and left him a small inheritance. Life on Charing Cross Road had become somewhat overstimulating and Derek was looking for a place to be quieter. He had a friend who lived on the shingle at Dungeness, that pocket of southern England that sounded to me so tantalisingly Scottish, the 'dangerous nose', the Fifth Quarter of the globe...

We drove along the shore road and stopped to skim flat stones like flints into the waves, pocket a few pebbles that we found with perfect holes in them, little knowing that this would be the first of a thousand afternoons for us spent in much the same way.

As we were turning to drive back to London, we saw, at the same moment, a small black-painted wooden house with yoke-yellow window frames on the left hand side of the road facing the sea. It had a 'For Sale' sign stuck in the stones at its feet. I remember distinctly turning in without a word and stopping the car.

We knocked on the door, were let in by the charming lady who lived there and after a tour that cannot have lasted longer than fifteen minutes, were back on the road heading north.

Derek decided before we reached Lydd that he would buy it.

And within a couple of months, was taking down chintz curtains and prising open the lid of the first of gazillion gallons of pitch black paint with which to anoint his new kingdom.

The pleasure he took in transforming this modest bungalow into the Tardis he created, the setting for his films, his books, his garden, the solace of the sea and the peculiar glamour of the nuclear power station (!), especially at the moment at which he discovered himself ill... is incalculable.

He made of this wee house, his wooden tent pitched in the wilderness, an art work – and out of its shingle skirts, an ingenious garden – now internationally recognised. But, first and foremost, the cottage was always a living thing, a practical toolbox for his work.

One Sunday, in London, I met Derek for lunch and he showed me with great ceremony, a piece of fabric he had bought that morning at Camden Lock: a fabulously rich and dense swathe of woven cream which he kept repeating he had paid a thousand pounds for.

'This is the start of the film', he kept saying. The fact of this eye-watering investment sealed in his mind his commitment to making a piece of work that started with an image of Jesus – or more particularly, Jesus' headdress – and the fantasy of this fabric photographed against the stones at Dungeness ignited a new film for him.

Over the next year, we shot, sporadically, both documentary sequences and set scenes in and around the cottage for the film that would become *The Garden*. But however drawn we were by the narrative element of Derek's scenarios – the Virgin harassed by and fighting down the paparazzi, the leatherdom Devil with whips and chains by halogen light, the pink-suited bridal Adam and Adam tender in parental bliss – it was the landscape of Dungeness that always drew us on.

The wind and the buffeted shrubs, the sea and the salt-weathered boats. The territory, this fifth quarter, planted the story of one (or other) Fisher of Men in a timeless reality worthy of Derek's great master, Pasolini. It was, in fact, the fabric of the place that brought that reality to Derek's fullest attention, beyond the glories of the Saviour's robe.

Derek – memorably – said that he would prefer his works after his death to evaporate and disappear. Beyond all the plaques, there are some places that offer the vision of a continued evolution as a point of encouragement and metaphysical enlightenment. I suggest that Prospect Cottage and Dungeness itself is such a place. It proved to be Jarman's heart's home, and the trusty generator of his work, as it ever has – and promises to continue to be – for countless others.

Olivia Laing *On Land, At Sea*

Damp October, a mist that doesn't lift all day. The air is full of water. My socks are soaked after a few minutes. Morning tasks: strip the ivy off a wall, lift a decaying deutzia, plant the clematis 'Alionushka'. Each job spawns others. Digging exposes the white runners of enchanter's nightshade, which need to be lifted out, and masses of bulbs, which need to be tucked back in, or divided and moved. Cutting back acanthus I find a daphne, daughter plant to the enormous Daphne bhoula 'Jacqueline Postill' that burns all winter, a tower of scent.

We were talking this morning about how it feels increasingly as if the internet is draining everything real out of the world. The sense of being trained by the algorithm, writhing around trying to please a force that is not visible and is difficult to understand. The garden is a place outside that. It has a different relationship to time, at once immediate and circular. What, I wonder as I'm digging, was Derek doing on this day. He writes about rain on taxi windows, writes later: "The rain has brought green back into my view."

In a world where everyone shares everything, it feels as if even inspiration is running a little thin. I covet Derek's hermetic vision, the sense that he was travelling in a private universe, sometimes alone and sometimes accompanied, but never in a crowd. Following a train of correspondences through centuries, a trail discernible to one, singular sensibility. Bombers pass overhead, a pilgrim mutters a prayer. Pasolini, Nash, Marlowe, dropping through time like a stone. The flowers are links in a chain, small portals. Heartsease, viola odorata, growing up from the medieval pharmacopeia gathered by Culpeper and Gerard.

I want to live wild inside time, old time, time that whirls you up with it. I think it's gone but it's still recoverable. The door stands open. The spell is called absorption, the spell is called concentration; opening out, becoming porous, and then distilling and distilling. It's still possible to enter the magic universe. "At Prospect I noticed thousands of seedlings had germinated in every nook and cranny." Tomorrow I'll plant a dahlia. Next week manure the beds, next month plant a peach, which will fruit in the summer and may yet outlive me.

Howard Sooley *Prospect Cottage*

Philip Hoare *Stormy weather*

"Friday 3 February 1989. I was describing the garden to Maggi Hambling at a gallery opening. And said I intended to write a book about it. She said: 'Oh, you've finally discovered nature, Derek.' 'I don't think it's quite like that,' I said, thinking of Constable and Samuel Palmer's Kent. 'Ah, I understand completely. You've discovered *modern nature*'."

Derek Jarman's *Modern Nature* is of course a future paradox now since, as we know, the one is rapidly obliterating the other. Written in a shingle desert at the end of England, Jarman's journals, published in 1991, three years before his death at the age of fifty-two, announced the beginning and ending of an era. His Prospect Cottage, strewn about by his bleak, beautiful garden in Dungeness was itself an ambivalent prospect. As if, held into the grey Channel, that elbow of land was a kind of barometer, like the nearby 'Listening Wall', an acoustic mirror built on the beach to detect enemy bombers. But now its concrete was sprayed with graffito announcing the Lion of Judah, Haile Selassie, and it was receiving other news, coming in on the wind and the tide.

A change in the weather.

From his four rooms there on the shore, Jarman looked to a future that was already in his head, in his art, in his apocalyptic films. *Jubilee* as cine verité; *The Garden* a natural history documentary scripted out of one of Albrecht Dürer's visionary engravings; *The Last of England* not a dream, but a waking nightmare.

This land became desert six hundred years ago when the sea rolled away. Since then it had been one of the driest, quietest places in England. Until Jarman arrived, followed by the Great Storm of 1987. That night whirled round him, as if he were at the centre of it all. He thought his wooden cabin might be taken up into the sky like Dorothy's house in *The Wizard of Oz*. But in the calm light of the morning, in the grey dawn, it seemed as though nothing had changed.

"Prospect stood firm on its foundations", he wrote. But the power was cut, and at night the blocky, eastern-bloc reactors glowed from inside, mocking the darkness inflicted on his cottage. And Derek's own body, already under assault from within, seemed to have become a conduit, a conductor. He had become a character from one of his films, as he had always been, the way that they were all a kind of fantastical autobiography, a flickering fancy dress. Caravaggio, Sebastiane, Prospero. Ariel, flying round the world, weaving dreams of past and future. The blasted shore, haunted by his own sense of possibilities: of being what he had done, and what he might yet do. That he might yet be released.

We all of us might be forgiven for feeling haunted these days. In his book *Humankind*, the radical philosopher Timothy Morton proposes a new relationship with nature for the future: a liberation from the "patriarchal, hierarchal, heteronormative possibility space... a highly necessary queering". Reviewing Morton's book, Stuart Jefferies wrote, "For Morton, our task is to become haunted beings again, possessed by a spectral sense of our connectedness to everything on this planet".

Derek's modern nature did not mean despair. Far from being dejected, abject, or passively accepting, his future haunting was a positive, pragmatic way of being, in the same way that his peer, the writer W.G. Sebald, regarded melancholy as a creative state, particularly when played out next to the sea; or that Dürer's androgynous watery angel in *Melencolia I*, clad in a damask gown and surrounded by the alchemical elements of their fate, looked up into the moonlit night and saw a comet bursting in the sky.

The angel as director as magician, lit by Josef von Sternberg. Jarman in his djellaba, turning the dark mirror on himself. As Michael Bracewell wrote, Jarman "employed an awareness of magic which he linked to both the technical processes of film-making and a semi-mystical sense of art". But it was a modernist magic, as Bracewell notes; and Jarman liked to think of the alchemy of Marcel Duchamp. He was a tourist from the future, wielding a black Claude glass or John Dee's obsidian disk and a cine camera, reflecting what lay ahead of us and focusing on what we had already lost. Far from pessimistic Jarman, for all his anger at the status quo, was a determined optimist; almost a conservative figure, even in his insurrection. Like Oscar Wilde, he was forever setting off for a new utopian shore, and failing to find it, sailing away again. The garden of Eden. Jarman=Garden, interchangeable, euphonious prospects. Before the original sin.

I feared Jarman's sinful films as a teenager. They disrupted my suburban world. Down here in the south coast of England, on an inlet, they were as scary as the sea beyond. It took me thirty years to learn to swim. Waiting for modern nature to come along. It is in his writing about his garden, and his gardening around his art, that I appreciated his spirit, because it is at its most intense there, in his sense of place. Jarman created something even more personal out of the past and its darkness. It's almost as if his art has continued to develop, like the darkly luminous photographs of it by Howard Sooley which were published in *Derek Jarman's*

Garden in 1995. By then Derek had been dead those twelve months, but the book, and Sooley's transcendent depth-of-field images reverberated with that past, echoing, in their archival modernity, with Jarman's origins in the mid-twentieth century. Born in 1942, he had grown up in an age when bombsites still pitted London and Southampton and other cities, their carved-out holes and rubble caves sprouting rosebay willowherb and purple buddleia as nature tried to reclaimed what was hers. Meanwhile there was a new, invisible cloud looming in the air: the radioactive traces of the first nuclear explosions that would contaminate the infant prelapsarian Derek's bones, and those of everyone else. We'd never be the same again, as a species. We'd been transformed, by an atomic Ariel.

This sense of an ending appears vividly in the neo-romantic painters of the period: artists such as John Minton, Graham Sutherland, John Piper, and Keith Vaughan. Their work distilled an unsettling dystopia, but also a biomorphic resistance. The body becomes the land, enacted upon, sensual, enigmatic, entangled; changing shape, space and time; resisting, persisting. Having trained at the Slade School of Art in the early nineteen-sixties, Jarman could not but be affected by their work, and that of more obscure figures such as Denton Welch, whose paintings and drawings and journals draw on his own disability (result of a near-fatal accident when cycling from Blackheath in 1935), his cool, ever-observing eye, watching boys bathing in a Kentish river or wartime bombers fly overhead.

Welch – later beloved of William Burroughs and John Waters for his lustrous, unapologetic sexuality – presented a priestly figure himself, dressing in a cassock and living as a semi-rural, semi-suburban aesthete in the fitful afterglow of empire and dissolution (born in China, his childhood memories echoing Jarman's); his own body rendered pathetic by his emasculated state and that of the broken world. In his imaginary state, drawing as he lay in his cottage, often in bed, Welch created still lives of entwined shells, mermaid-like creatures impaled on spears and disembodied hands. Faces grow cone-shaped vision or stare blind-eyed as statues, as if contorted with the real pain he felt.

In his writing and in his painting, Welch's mortal evocations of south-eastern England merge into two-dimensional stage sets and the end-papers of his books. Living with partner, and carer, Eric Oliver, he was photographed slumped on a fur rug, surrounded by his shells, looking languidly back at the camera as if seeing himself from above, "as two eyes looking down on my empty room, on my silent velvet bed, on all my pretty things, and knowing that I shall never use them again. I think of them floating into other people's homes and being used for a hundred years from hence."

Like Welch, who died in 1948 at the age of thirty-three, Derek Jarman's art and life connects that reverberation of blitzkrieg and fatalism – in the Home Counties skies or Welsh hills – with the new austerity, that of the nineteen-seventies. And just as punk would be born out of those ruins, so that sense of past and future destruction created its own artistic opposition. Jarman's RAF officer father, and his mother who looked as though she'd just stepped out of *Brief Encounter*; the comforting stasis of England, disrupted, ripped up by queer things; Derek riding pillion on a motorbike with his hands in the rider's trouser pockets, hanging on the handsome boy as much as to himself.

Jarman's own legitimate body, and what he would do with it; his sense of agency and urgency versus the illegitimacy imposed by the outside world, the unnatural versus his natural self. This sense of nature/artifice/performance is seeded in the faded colour of family home movies or the forties Technicolor of Powell and

Pressburger's films. You might imagine Jarman as the professor at the beginning of *A Matter of Life and Death* (1946), wielding the lens of his camera obscura to look out panoptically at the world going on around him. But he is also the French revolutionary dandy summoned from heaven, first seen in black and white until his rose buttonhole turns into a vivid pink. Another kind of magician.

These were new stories of metamorphosis: a boy in the dunes in the nude, playing a pipe as a man fallen from the sky stumbles onto the sand, seguing to the blowsy roses of Earl's Court, where Jarman buys his blooms, which in turn evoke family holidays in Italy, described in sensuous detail as scenes from the films of Fellini or Bertolucci or Pasolini. And all these memories were replete with "the timeless sadness of childhood" for Jarman, as he wrote in his journal, in a knowing evocation of what he sees as his "personal mythology" and "archaeology". The past, disinterred, still happening. The seaside suburbia of Milford-on-Sea and Barton in Hampshire where he was schooled; the Dancing Ledge of Dorset and the standing stones of Avebury that marked out his vision of the mystical past. Like Paul Nash's landscapes or John Banting's queer flowers or Eileen Agar's surreal assemblies of mutable marine debris, they're all sites of performance in which new identities might be seeded, future species emerging from the rubble and the shore.

And they in turn translate, these uneasy inheritances, as if filtered through Jarman's eye and his biography, to the images of his early films, made in the first half of the nineteen-seventies; celluloid artefacts replete with a luminous, innocent decadence and a sort of amniotic haze. Ritualistic, animated stained glass in fancy dress. The prehistoric road-trip of *A Journey to Avebury* (1971) charged with a Neolithic radiance and ancient sun. The re-enactment of some weird watery fable in *At Low Tide* (1972), in which ungendered bodies float in rock pools on the Dorset coast, emerging as monstrous monarchs of an aquatic realm. *Corfe Film* (1975), made in a nearby ruined castle, a Pre-Raphaelite Roxy Music dream. And *Fire Island (My Very Beautiful Movie)* (1974), set on a New England utopian shore where Wilde and Auden swam and Melville's *Billy Budd* was born.

They might all be scenes from a marvellous party seen through in the decayed light of the dead Thames, the artist's encampments on the bombed-out bankside. An antediluvian world, in the way that Howard Sooley's photographs would capture Jarman's Dungeness as somewhere before or after the flood, briefly revealed by the receding sea, a fantastical sea bed, before the waves rolled back in again. A brief interlude, even under the benthic pressure of oppression and hate. A potential utopia of its own; the dark retreats of the city, the lawlessness of the sea. A natural resistance for people told that they were themselves unnatural. Not admitting defeat.

Jarman knew all too well the way we rehearse our personal myths. He leads us from gardens where we feel secure to the cruising grounds of Hampstead, a bucolic landscape populated by Poussin satyrs in leather, and from there to the edge of withdrawing sea of faith on Dungeness's dangerous shore, where Keith Collins, Derek's life partner, known to him as Hinney Beast, told me it was too dangerous to swim – not on account of the high Geiger count, but because of other unseen currents that run deep and strong there. That's where Jarman came to an end, where England ran out. Any shore defies laws, since it is where laws run out. But it is also where they begin, as refugees now arriving on that shore discover to their cost. They find no utopia there.

Reading *Modern Nature* in the nineteen-nineties – and many times again since – Jarman's journals made me feel bereft of London, almost as if the city had already died. I had found it increasingly hard to take. The acuteness of Jarman's retreat from the hedonistic brilliance of his years from 1975 to 1985 was my experience too. At first in an imaginary, secondhand manner, in the way I rummaged for dead men and women's clothes in jumble sales on dark winter evenings in my Southampton suburb; then actually, as I was willingly sucked into the metropolis's dark underbelly as I moved to London in 1976, drawn there by the spirit of the starman whom I saw on stage at the beginning of that year, singing out of the dark arena, throwing darts in lover's eyes; and by the punk clubs in a then derelict Covent Garden to which I would descend at that year's end to see the Vibrators perform in lurex drainpipes and platform boots, watched, unbeknown to me, by Marianne Faithfull who had married their lead singer. Punk blew up out of decay and rot. It was a new home to me. Sometime in early 1977 I was shown a film script by the photographer Peter-Paul Hartnett, who suggested I might like an extra's role in it. I thought it looked absurd, and turned down the offer. It was *Jubilee.*

But it was telling that three years later, on a beach close to Dungeness's shore, the starman was filmed in Jarmanesque baroqueness singing, 'Ashes to Ashes', a vampire neurosis in which his pierrot, neo-romantic-clad body out of a padded cell, floundered there in an irradiated sea, not waving but drowning, all the while accompanied by escapees from the not-unironically named Blitz club. Jarman had wanted the starman to appear in his projected film, *Neutron*, just as he'd hoped he would to play or sing Ariel for *The Tempest.* I ran through these imaginary scenarios in my head; and even years later, when a friend told me of the sensation created when the starman and Jarman were seen walking up Charing Cross Road together, still felt a sense of deep longing for something I could not regret.

•

On the Ness, the weeds are allowed to be themselves. Outsiders, outriders. Arrayed with stones, and sustained by poor soil if any at all. Jarman played with the first piece of land he had had under his cultivation since he was a child. Set at this centre of Jarmanworld™, was his hut, its timbers tarred against the weather, if not the climate, which was already displaying symptoms of breaking down. Like Edward Carpenter's cottage outside

Sheffield, or Henry David Thoreau's hut on the shores of Walden Pond, or even the Dieppe beach hut housing a driftwood Madonna which Wilde had built on the far shore of the Channel, to which he proceeded directly on his discharge from Reading Gaol. Or whatever seaweedy subliminal structure Prospero erected on his magical island of strange noises.

At the end of a century that sometimes seemed to be going in reverse, it was no coincidence that Jarman called it Prospect Cottage, or that the nineteen-thirties moderne apartment block that contained his London flat – a tiny dark roomed set of cubby-like rooms opposite St Martin's School of Art – was named Phoenix House after the Phoenix Theatre over which it sat. (The state-of-the-art auditorium had been the site of the 1930 premiere of Noël Coward's play, *Private Lives*, and of Coward's *The Vortex*, in whose revival Jarman's wickedly handsome friend Rupert Everett starred. Jarman noted of the play that its theme of cocaine abuse was a mask for the dramatist's masked desires. Coward 'put his sexuality in a little silver box and sniffed it', he wrote in *Modern Nature*.)

Straddling Soho and Charing Cross, intersectional places, alleys and doorways which had for centuries been illicit trysting places – and where Marianne Faithfull, whose devastating song of attrition, 'Broken English', was filmed by Jarman on the same streets on which she had lived for two years as an addicted, anorexic fallen angel – Phoenix House's city sooty bricks and Crittall windows seemed similarly resurrected: from the Great

Fire or dug up from the plague pit under St Anne's churchyard as much as from the Blitz. Or perhaps this was where Quatermass's nineteen-fifties aliens landed, demon gargoyles creeping out of their pod in their Knightsbridge crater. And hence the silver witch ball which Jarman hung in the window, acting, like the hag stones he hung around the necks of visitors to Dungeness to ward off evil, as Jon Savage told me, sporting his talisman in the streets of downtown New York.

By that time I too had retreated to the shore, adapting to another life, by a similarly shingly sea, sown with the same plants, and the same debris, overlooking by a refinery, a power station, and the ghosts of the past yet to come. Storms, as Pet Shop Boys sang, blow themselves out. *Modern Nature* created just that: a vision of modern nature. A heightened sensibility – allying the natural world to his 'unnatural' world – that in some ways recalls the Victorian writer, Richard Jefferies, who struggled against disease to create a perfervid, highly personal account of the fragile rurality of southern England, at a time when it was seriously under threat from industrialisation. Like Walt Whitman, Jefferies sensed the body of the earth beneath its skin and his own. He's ecstatic, almost orgasmic in his time-travelling moment of witness.

"Give me still more", Jefferies wrote, in *The Story of My Heart*, in 1883, "for the interminable universe, past and present, is but earth." He even imagined, in his book, *After London; or, Wild England*, the city in an undefined post-apocalyptic state in which nature creeps back in, reversing the process of suburbanisation, colonising its wrecked state, the way that silver birch and buddleia become the advance guard of a newly liberated place. "It became green everywhere, in the first spring, after London ended", wrote Jefferies. "When the ancients departed."

•

Jarman's journals are forever collecting, images and things. So too the paintings he created around his cottage are beachcombed, drawn from the shore, and from his memory. "We lit the bonfire with driftwood and boiled up the tar as the sun set", he writes, on 1 August 1989. "In the gathering shadows we completed new paintings: a mirrored Coke can surrounded by demons; and a ship in a bottle – filled with black gold and smashed." Like the folk art 'gods-in-bottles' – enigmatic wooden objects swelling in tobacco-coloured water, created by nineteenth-century Irish immigrants to Britain – these are rituals as much as art. "The glass fell on to the canvas like a tallship in full sail; the tar eddied about it, the broken masts of the ship swallowed in black – black that breaks down forms and distinctions, swallows shadows."

Those paintings pour out, uncontained, indiscriminate, stilled, reminiscent of the most homoerotic scene in nineteenth-century literature, in *Moby-Dick*, when Melville's sailors, enlisting in Ahab's monomanical campaign to revenge himself on the great white whale that bit off his leg – and, as Melville clearly suggests, his manhood, too – the crew of the *Pequod* sit round a tub of spermaceti oil harvested from a leviathan's head, squeezing each other's hands in a sensual reverie. "The hot tar splashed everywhere", Jarman writes, "and set like shining jet."

The pitch paintings challenge blind faith in their shards of glass and impressed objects or holy texts, rendered illegible and impotent like a tarred cormorant, anthropogenic bycatch of a nightmarish oil spill. They're naked and explicit. Their power is in the fact that their gestures (sometimes naïve as they are), remain, freeze-framed, now that they are needed more than ever. The artist stands back, hands in boilersuit pockets. St Derek's insouciance is part of his charm.

It's almost cute. That big smile.

Art, Warhol said, it whatever you can get away with. All art, as Timothy Morton says, is from the future. None of it is in the past. Jarman could not know what was coming, but he forecast it in the incorporation of plastic debris from the sea in his assemblages receive their footnote, as I write, as scientists announce that the polymer plastics which have now entered the fossil record date back to the nineteen-forties, the decade of Jarman's birth. (I'm not blaming him).

These works are Dada/punk/Kiefers-by-the-sea, blackened and burnt-out like TWOC'd cars. They're natural histories turned inside-out, in the way his nature had been proclaimed unnatural for half his life. These are action paintings are protests, still lives arrested by his *nature morte*. They're tarry epitaphs, but also traps for unwary megafauna, lurching prejudices, like giant sloths and mastodons. And all these scenes are seen through standing stones, dragon's teeth buried in the ground, filmed by Jarman on his sixteenth-century Super 8 camera. After all, the celluloid on which he filmed derived from the same petro-chemical processes – and as in the recent past, its gelatine had been processed from dead whales, filtering a fatal light, in the way that, as James Mackay notes, cinema projectionists from the interwar period would open up the back of their projectors while the film was running and get their white bodies tanned by the ultraviolet rays.

Refined, transforming. Jarman's *Glitterbug* Thames-side seventies decadence and the greenhouse effect of his Butler's Wharf hothouse. The little magical mirrors used to capture and deflect the sun. Psychic geo-engineering. A dark territory ruled over by symbolical women of power and transformation in Jarman's films, played by Tilda Swinton, Elisabeth Welch, Jordan, Jenny Runacre. The white robe that Jarman found, almost miraculously, in Camden Market, as Tilda recalled, that became the Pasolini totem for the making of *The Garden*.

And just as Melville turns whiteness into something appalling in *Moby-Dick*, so Jarman turns blackness into something enthralling like the moment when the guides take their visitors deep into a cave and turn the lights off, revealing a primal darkness that is actually tactile. The illicit darkness of the Heath, as yet unlit by the zombie glow of mobile phones. The fugitive alleys and dives of Soho and the dark-flowing Thames. The matt black caverns of Heaven, and in its saturnalia, where I last saw him, chatting away with him, knowing I'd already written his obituary. The absolute darkness of the sea and sky seen, through his window overlooking an endless beach.

Darkness out of light. Defined.

•

Before I wrote this, before 'all of this', myself and my fellow curators got locked into Prospect Cottage, the way we used to get locked into East End pubs. Outside it was a bleak November day, a good day for coffins in warehouses or for laying-out the table in the sun room with its creator's corpse, as they lay Jarman there for his wake. Now he lay in the nearby medieval churchyard, lurching over the edge of the turf, as if to greet the sea which will soon be rolling it, joined by Keith Collins, his Hinney Beast. His body was laid on top of his friend's.

Meanwhile, in the cottage, where Collins lately complained, resignedly of art tourists peering in through the windows and catching him in his pants, the house, a Tardis of eight rooms that seemed to expand the more we walked around, was darkened and silent. A life-size cardboard image of Tilda Swinton stood in one corner, her seraphic face advertising a *Time Out* interview on the artist. On a shelf next to

Toyah Wilcox's tiara from *The Tempest* lay Jarman's hand-held cine camera. Strange to look at that machine, so resolutely analogue, like a toy, rather than an extension of his eye. In the glazed bookcase stood a quartet of cheap plaster busts bought from charity shops, their heads knocked off and replaced with hag stones or wound round with wire. They were still lined up there as if for sale – Prospect Products, as Keith joked, as if his partner had become a cottage industry.

It all suddenly felt so fragile, in the oncoming night. Terribly intimate, given how public much of Jarman's life was. Not always by choice. A man alternately savaged, acclaimed and redeemed; who became a kind of middle-class acquisition of daring culture, in the way Wilde and Coward were adopted, only to be carried away by the last unprecedented pandemic. Jarman's modern nature persists precisely because of his resistance and his generosity. The visitors stumble across the shingle in awe and wonder at what this man showed to the world.

The autumn afternoon turned to evening. The mauve light came in through the window of Jarman's study overlooking the sea, invisible on the horizon. His desk was still littered with his pens and a repurposed plastic figurine of the Incredible Hulk sitting astride a worm-bored rock. The day failed us. The night came on. I turned away from his room and said sorry for interrupting him.

The three of us stepped out into the blue night and shut the door.

Derek Jarman *Super 8 film stills*

A Journey to Avebury, 1971

At Low Tide, 1972

My Very Beautiful Movie, 1974

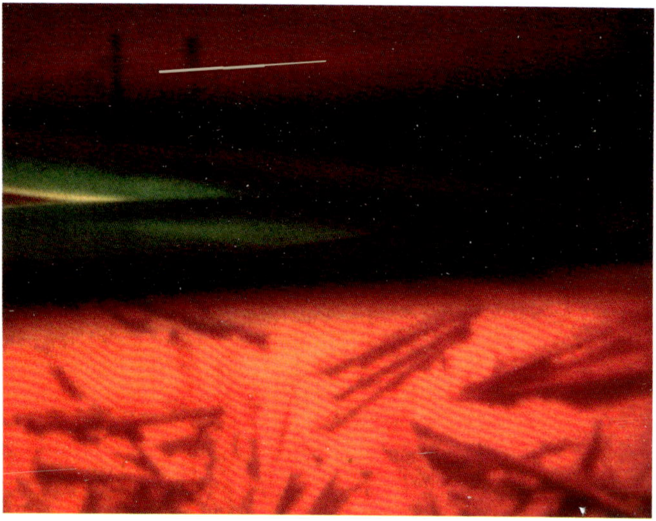

Corfe Film, 1975

Liam Daniel *The Garden*, 1990

Neil Tennant *Derek Jarman*

Derek was a constant presence in my life for six or seven years and I think about him often. When you go to Dungeness there is a powerful atmosphere of him in the house. I used to see his big black sketchbooks open on his desk filled with his beautiful script. There was something medieval about Derek, sitting in the house at Dungeness in this wood-panelled room. He looked like a monk in the 13th century – doing calligraphy or copying out the works of St Augustine. There was something weirdly ecclesiastical about him and he was very methodical and practical, like almost every creative person I have ever known.

When I first met Derek, he had just discovered he was HIV positive. People forget now but at this time it was thought that if you were HIV positive you had about a 50 per cent chance of getting 'full-blown' AIDS. My best friend, who I'd known since I was a kid in Newcastle, never went through being HIV positive. He just got AIDS, lived another three years and then died. Politically we were in Mrs Thatcher's third term and our album *Actually* was partly intended as an anti-Thatcherite statement: 'Shopping' was about the nationalised industries being sold off; 'King's Cross' was about the victims of Thatcherism. Our earlier song 'Opportunities' – which had the lyrics "I've got the brains, you've got the looks. Let's make lots of money" – was also a satire of Thatcherism. This was a time when the money culture had really kicked in and Harry Enfield spoofed it with his 'Loadsamoney' character. It was the high point of triumphant Thatcherism and we were also in the early years of AIDS.

Derek was pretty famous. When *Sebastiane* (1976) came out it was quite a big deal, being in Latin and with the nudity. I saw it but, at this point, the only other films of his I had seen were the pop promos he had made with Marianne Faithfull and The Smiths. In 1987 Chris Lowe and I were making 'It's a Sin' at the Advision studio behind Oxford Street and while we were mixing the record *Caravaggio* (1986) was on television on Channel 4. It looked great and we had the idea to ask Derek Jarman to direct our video. I knew by then that Derek made films on low budgets and we wanted to do something that looked like a movie but wouldn't cost hundreds of thousands of pounds. Anyway, someone got in touch with Derek and he came over to the studio the next day with a team of people. My recollection is that Cerith Wyn Evans [artist and Jarman's film assistant] was there, wearing a sort of Vivienne Westwood kilt. Derek assumed we wanted to do the video in Super 8 and he was quite surprised when Chris and I said that wasn't what we had in mind.

First we played him the record because we'd literally just finished it and we were very proud of it – it sounded amazing, huge and ridiculous. Anyway we said we want to do the video like Caravaggio. I had the idea that I wanted to be burnt at the stake at the end. I always romanticised Joan of Arc because of my Catholic upbringing and I had this camp idea that I'd be burnt at the stake. Then Chris, myself and Derek and his team discussed it and how much it was going to cost. I later read in Derek's diaries a remark that he had more money to make the video than he would get for one of his films. My recollection is that we had £70,000; for us that was a lot of money although there were people spending more. I always admired the fact that Derek made films on very low budgets that were still shown at the cinema.

It was a good meeting; I remember thinking how affable he was and not really what I expected. I was expecting someone who was more self-conscious but Derek had this very chatty, enthusiastic personality, laughing a lot. He also had this part of him that was full of anger, which I think fuelled his film work, so he had different sides to his personality.

We made the video for 'It's a Sin' at Bankside, which had recently been used as the set for Stanley Kubrick's war film *Full Metal Jacket* (1987). There was still stuff from the film lying around. We were thrilled by all the actors who appeared in cameos in 'It's a Sin', such as Ron Moody who had played Fagin in *Oliver!* Later Derek made another video for us: 'Rent' which Margi Clarke appeared in.

In 1988 Jon Savage and I drove down to Dungeness to see Derek, who'd recently moved into his fisherman's cottage there, and we stopped off at Rye which I immediately fell in love with and where six months later I bought a house. I was very impressed by Dungeness, at how wild it was and also by Derek's spartanness. My home in Rye was very bourgeois compared to Derek's but I loved his house. After I bought the house in Rye, we used to go to Dungeness quite often. We'd sit in the garden and drink Earl Grey tea from the Algerian Coffee House on Old Compton Street and eat cakes and chat.

I wasn't 'out' at this point, but I wasn't 'in' either. I didn't have pretend girlfriends and I didn't pretend to be straight. I never said I was gay because I always thought it more interesting when for fans your sexuality is a matter of mystery rather than defined publicly.

By 1989 we had sold a lot of records and we had this big offer to tour in Japan and we asked Derek to put the show together and direct it. We had the idea, which is beyond commonplace now but it was unusual in those days, to have film projected behind us. We thought Derek could do everything – costumes, film, the sets – because we knew he's directed an opera and worked in the theatre. In Derek's account of all this in his diary there's a sense that he doesn't completely know what he's doing and is winging it slightly, which is always exciting. Directing an arena rock show was something that was quite outside his experience. I remember him phoning me up from the editing suite, laughing with excitement, and saying that this was the first time anyone had ever blown up Super 8 to 35 mm.

One afternoon in Dungeness we discussed ideas for the tour production, going through it song by song. It was a gorgeous afternoon; the light down there is so bright and we all sat outside drinking tea, the costume designer sketching and Derek making notes. There was a fantastic sequence for 'It's a Sin' with amazing costumes for each of the seven deadly sins. It was a corny idea but very successful. Before it we played this track called 'The Sound of the Atom Splitting', the lyrics of which were inspired by a line in *The Last of England* (1987). It was a really great sequence. When the show was ready, we went to Hong Kong and Japan and we decided to do it in Britain afterwards. When it opened, the music press loved it, although the broadsheets were a bit slaggy. Derek came to the gigs in Britain.

After the tour in 1989 we didn't really work with Derek again, although we did a couple of performances for him. When *Edward II* (1991) premiered in London, he asked us to play at the premiere party at Heaven nightclub. Then in 1992, Derek had an art exhibition at Manchester City Art Gallery and we performed for him at the Hacienda, which was when we first performed our cover version of 'Go West' by The Village People.

Derek was an important anti-Thatcherite figure; at the same time as being an artist, he had a strong political agenda. I think that was because of AIDS and probably also because of Clause 28. You could regard his opinions as extreme but at the time there was a lot to be angry about. There's a cliché about the 1980s that it was all about money but when you look back it was also an incredibly bohemian, alternative period. Boy George and Culture Club came from an alternative scene and entered the mainstream. We came from an alternative background but went super mainstream. The mainstream, of course, feeds on the alternative; now the mainstream doesn't have an alternative to feed on anymore. The same was true of theatre and cinema, the idea that you can make Super 8 films like *The Last of England* or *The Garden* (1990) and get them shown at big cinemas, which is unthinkable now really because everything's leaning towards Hollywood and everything is about money. What united us with Derek was being against the money culture, which we're still against and Derek would still be against. His diaries are a historically important record of his anger at what was happening in Britain at the time and how politicised the gay world was.

Being on set with Derek there was a happy atmosphere, very different to a normal video director. It was more relaxed but also slightly nervy because he was working it out while he was doing it. It was much more bohemian than the regular pop shoot. He embodied these two worlds colliding. For the 'Rent' video I played a chauffeur who drives Margi Clarke from a posh dinner party to pick up a boy, possibly her brother (played by Chris Lowe), from King's Cross station. Derek knew someone who owned this big house, behind the Mall and he filmed the dinner party scene there.

In 1990 Derek told me that the 90s were all going to be about gardening for him and he created the extraordinary garden at Dungeness and also shot his film *The Garden* there. The garden was maybe his most 'Jarman-esque' creation and became very famous and, in its own way, influential. Whenever I see pebbles in a boutique hotel I think, thanks Derek!

Derek was one of the last three people I knew who died of AIDS, all in 1994 before the drug combination treatment came through. If he'd hung on for another year, he would still be here. I saw him in hospital not long before he died and he talked about making *Blue* (1993). He said he was making a film about being blind and he was laughing about it. He would sit surrounded by all these bottles of drugs and we used to discuss how beautiful the packaging was – the pastel colours and lovely typography. In *Blue* there's a point where the narrator reads out all the side effects of the drugs and at the screening I remember people laughing, including Derek. He had this macabre sense of humour. The last time I saw him was when he was in St Bartholomew's Hospital. He was suffering but he was still talking about projects.

In the few years that I knew Derek, he made films and paintings but there was also his political activism, the diaries, the garden, the house. It's a powerful and unique body of work and I was privileged to know him and inspired by him.

Ali Smith *Mr J*

To make a garden in a stony place. To understand the wildness in the garden. To grow a garden up against the odds – so up against the wall that the wall falls. To open up a garden, instead of close it in. To suggest that garden and horizon are the same. God, I'm glad to have lived to see a time when films and art and vision like Derek Jarman's changed the story, opened up the story, made it more liveable, natural, wild, wise, fierce, and joyous with a passionate and revolutionary warmth that was an open threshold to how to live and love and see the world and see each other.

In a time of deep institutional and traditional hostilities he knew tradition differently. When he was in the room, or in the art, it was like what he did shrugged off the centuries, the rags of their preconceptions, everything that makes a person less than a person is.

The first flower he planted in his garden, legend has it, was a dog-rose dug up elsewhere in Dungeness. No way it would take. Wind, stone and rain. But it did. Nothing stops the natural from happening.

There's a famous Norwegian poet from a couple of centuries ago who died young and whose last words come to mind whenever I think of Jarman and the space he made for us with his radical geniality and all its bright demeanour.

Kiss next year's roses for me.

Why we're here: to make sure next year's roses lift their heads and open in an open garden.

The gift of him against the odds: the lean of a sprig against a gale, still flowering.

Acknowledgements

Through the process of curating this exhibition, we have enjoyed the privilege of visiting Prospect Cottage in Dungeness and had the pleasure of working with Derek Jarman's friends and colleagues. We are particularly indebted to Keith Collins (1966–2018) and the Keith Collins Will Trust. We would especially like to thank the Trustees: Diane Gelon, Karl Lydon, Amanda Wilkinson, for their tireless dedication in realising Keith Collins' wishes and promoting Derek Jarman's legacy.

John Hansard Gallery would firstly like to express deepest thanks to our co-curator, editor and contributor to this publication, Philip Hoare, who has been an inspiration from the moment the idea for *Derek Jarman's Modern Nature* first seeded itself. Philip's limitless drive, enthusiasm and passion have made both the exhibition and this publication possible. We would also like to extend especial thanks to Amanda Wilkinson, who has been an invaluable source of help, guidance and advice throughout. Utmost thanks is due to all the artists in the exhibition: Maggi Hambling, Richard Porter, Tanoa Sasraku, Howard Sooley, Wolfgang Tillmans, Sarah Wood; and all the contributors to this publication: Philip Hoare, Olivia Laing, James Mackay, Ali Smith, Howard Sooley, Tilda Swinton, Alexandra Symons Sutcliffe, Neil Tennant, and designers Wayne Daly and Claire Lyon; who have all given so generously of their time and energy.

A sincere thank you to all lenders and representatives of collections and estates, including: Amanda Wilkinson Gallery; Keith Collins Will Trust; James Mackay, Basilisk Communications, LUMA Foundation; The Art Fund, Creative Folkestone (Stephen Deuchar, Alistair Upton); Southampton City Art Gallery (Dan Matthews, Clare Mitchell, Rebecca Moisan); The Ingram Collection (Jo Baring, Alison Price); IAP Fine Art (David Tregunna); Martin Thomas; Maureen Paley; Tara Ferry; Neil Tennant; Michael Garbett. Special thanks also to: Jonny Bruce; Tate Archive; Eye Film; Halo; Sean Kissane; Fiona Corridan; and all staff at John Hansard Gallery.

Image credits

Cover
Derek Jarman on the set of *The Garden*, 1990. Photograph: Liam Daniel. Courtesy and © Basilisk Communications

p 23
Illustration of a violet from John Gerard's *Herbal*, first published 1597

pp 27–38
Photographs of the garden and portraits of Derek Jarman at Prospect Cottage, Dungeness. Photographs: Howard Sooley

p 41
Elisabeth Welch, *Stormy Weather*, 1980, Industrial Records

p 43
Albrecht Dürer, *Melencolia I*, 1514, engraving

p 46
Denton Welch, *A Voice Through a Cloud*, endpapers, 1950

p 59
Prospect Cottage, Dungeness, November 2019. Photograph: Philip Hoare

pp 62–69
Super 8 film stills:
Derek Jarman, *A Journey to Avebury*, 1971; Derek Jarman, *At Low Tide*, 1972; Derek Jarman, *My Very Beautiful Movie*, 1974; Derek Jarman, *Corfe Film*, 1975. All courtesy and © The LUMA Foundation

pp 72–79
Production stills from *The Garden*, dir. Derek Jarman, 1990. Photographs: Liam Daniel. Courtesy and © Basilisk Communications

Published on the occasion of
the exhibition:
Derek Jarman's Modern Nature
27 November 2021–26 February 2022
John Hansard Gallery, University
of Southampton

A John Hansard Gallery exhibition,
curated with Philip Hoare

Director: Woodrow Kernohan

Exhibition team: Ros Carter,
Nadia Thondrayen, Lee Broughall

Technical team: Julian Grater,
Josef Hill, Amy Scott-Pillow

Engagement team: Lynne Dick,
Dianna Djokey, Kat Henderson

Communications and Marketing:
Jack Lewis, Four Communications

Editor: Philip Hoare
Design: Daly & Lyon
Printing: Aldgate Press
Distribution: Cornerhouse
Publications, Manchester, UK

ISBN 978-1-912431-15-1

Published by:
John Hansard Gallery
142–144 Above Bar Street
Southampton
SO14 7DU

www.jhg.art

Proceeds from the sale of this publication will be donated to Breakout Youth, an independent charity based in Hampshire and the Isle of Wight. Breakout Youth offers a confidential support service for young people aged 11 to 25, who are lesbian, gay, bisexual, transgender, questioning or unsure of their sexuality or gender identity.

897 / 1,000